SILENCE

A DIARY OF SUFFERING
AND REDEMPTION

ANTONY GABRIEL

WESTBOW
PRESS®
A DIVISION OF THOMAS NELSON
& ZONDERVAN

WestBow Press books may be ordered through booksellers or by contacting:

WestBow Press
A Division of Thomas Nelson & Zondervan
1663 Liberty Drive
Bloomington, IN 47403
www.westbowpress.com
1 (866) 928-1240

ISBN: 978-1-5127-9055-9 (sc)
ISBN:978-1-5127-9056-6 (hc)
ISBN: 978-1-5127-9054-2 (e)

Library of Congress Control Number: 2017909298

Print information available on the last page.

WestBow Press rev. date: 06/16/2017

To Lynn Gabriel and Sally Lou Ghiz—two angels.

If one does not understand my silence, neither will he understand my words.

—*Venerable Pambo, the Hermit of Egypt*

TABLE OF CONTENTS

FOREWORD

The Antony Gabriel is an endangered species: Storyteller, Poet, Historian, Observer of Humanity, Spiritual Father, Man of God, and all too often, just a regular human struggling with his faith and the overwhelming vicissitudes of life.

Part memoire and part spiritual journal, this cathartic book invites the reader to discover redemption in the midst of suffering. Along this painful journey, there are spiritual gems to be collected; especially in the second part of this book.

Antony Gabriel's sharp, clear memory and keen eye for detail gives us a virtual reality experience in words. If only, like some Vulcan Mind Meld, we could plug into his brain and see things through his eyes and feel through his big and scarred heart, we would then be able to experience the soul of this dear man of God.

This book reminds me of a small desert plant I was given. One day a wreath of beautiful fuchsia colored flowers blossomed as a crown encircling this prickly cactus. It reminded me that even in the desert times of our lives, flowers can bloom. Instead of the crown of thorns worn by our Lord during His passion, it is a crown of hope for a new and beautiful life. A victor's crown of triumph!

Like his namesake St Antony, through suffering comes a divine encounter with God that can only take place in the spiritual deserts of our lives. Antony Gabriel takes the reader on his triumphal "walk <u>through</u> the valley of the shadow of death" (Psalm 23:4) to arrive in the promised land of peace, joy, and love.

He sums up this book best: *"For those suffering can either be victim or victor. By faith in Jesus we are all victors!"*

George Taweel

PREFACE

In my previous book, *Gabriel's Dragon,* I described how I faced a major colon cancer operation in 1995. This little book tells the story of my further dramatic encounters with mortality. In a striking but unsettling example of synchronicity, I was in a coma at the same hospital when that book was released some eight years later.

The account of the six weeks I spent in a coma and the four months I subsequently spent at the hospital in 2003, suspended between life and death and unable to speak or to make sense of what had happened to me, became the book you are now reading and is the reason for its title, *Silence.* When I was at last able to grapple with what had happened, I started to scrawl notes on little pieces of paper. I would later assemble these bits of paper and have them transcribed into a journal, upon which this account of my experience has been based.

During that time, I bore my suffering as a silent witness. I did not ask God, "Why me?" At some level I understood that the question was not, "Why me?" but rather, "Why not me?" I thought maybe there was some use yet for this chief of all sinners. Perhaps God had kept me around for purposes other than my own narcissistic self.

I thought what I had gone through might possibly help others, as I tried to make sense of what had happened.

As a clergyman, I held a position of influence in the Antiochian Church of North America and particularly in the Montreal community. I have coped with the fragility of life, although until recently, mostly in the lives of others. Yet I too have dealt with my share of personal crises.

Even today, I have difficulty sharing this story. However, when someone invited me to speak to audiences in that difficult year following my slow, partial recovery, it helped me make sense of my ordeals. I believe it helped others to do the same. As I shared these experiences to promote healing by expressing my innermost feelings, it gave courage to others as well as birth to this book. So, while I am a clergyman who has encountered death face-to-face, this is a story for everyman.

On a most personal note, I also wish to remember my beloved brother Charles Elias Gabriel, who passed into eternity on February 15, 2017. Charles was my older brother, and not only were we siblings but best friends. We spoke together frequently; traveled together with our wives and our relationship will endure into all eternity.

We shared our bedrooms, paper routes and all the joys and tribulations of life. We worked together in the family grocery store and shared the *joie de vivre* and the journey to success in our prospective endeavors. He was also my protector, even as an adult, for when I was in a coma, as described in this book, it was to Charles that my wife Lynn turned to for comfort and help. He stayed by my bedside constantly and when my prognosis looked grim, he, as he told me later, demanded that God send me back!

In February 2017, my beloved brother's health failed. As I was preparing to go to the airport to be with him and his family in Syracuse, I was hospitalized for yet another bowel blockage.

Meanwhile, my sister Sharon rushed to Syracuse to be with Charles. Just before my brother left us, my sister placed the phone to his ear while I chanted the hymns of our Church to him from my hospital bed. "Brother, you can go now, God is waiting for you!" I told him. Later that evening he saw the Light, and left in peace in the loving arms of the Divinity.

Finally, I want to thank so many good friends who have helped in shaping the narrative called Silence; A Diary of Suffering and Redemption. For their encouragement and assistance, I am eternally grateful.

When your fear cometh as desolation, and your destruction cometh as a whirlwind; when distress and anguish cometh upon you. Then shall they call upon me, but I will not answer; they shall seek me early, but they shall not find me.

—Proverbs 1:27–28 (KJV)

PART 1

THE WHIRLWIND: THE APPALLING STRANGENESS OF GOD'S MERCY

This chapter of my life unfolded in June of 2003 as I tried to balance the demands of a busy parish and attend to the parish life and the community activities of St. George Antiochian Orthodox Church in Montreal. At the same time, I tried to maintain some semblance of normalcy as I kept appointments with various medical specialists to deal with the increasingly painful complications from what I thought was diverticulitis.[1]

I had had an operation for colon cancer in 1995. I had received the very best treatment, which is why I am here today. I'd had it all: chemotherapy, interferon, steroids, and almost every other potent, disease-combatting drug imaginable. As is often the case, the operation had been a success, but the patient had almost died.

To this day, I believe that the aggressive protocol—the combination of lethal chemicals that was used to combat my cancer during the six-month treatment that followed my surgery—weakened my immune system, which had already been compromised by a condition called Boeck's Sarcoidosis.[2] I continued to have health issues. These included a hemicolectomy, adhesions, diverticulitis, and other complications and were the catalysts for the recurring nightmare of surgeries, hospital stays, relapses, and infections, which had led to yet more hospital stays.

I had been sent to Montreal some forty years earlier, when I was a young priest with a family, to minister at the parish of St. George. It was a mixture of recent immigrant families who brought the divisions of their homelands with them and establishment Montrealers. It reflected the major social fault lines of Montreal society. Now there are added factions and politics, which come with the ever-present drama of events in the Middle East overshadowing the business of parish life.

The parish had grown, and the business of running it sometimes seemed to consume all my energies. Management of a multilingual, multi-ethnic parish: looking after the spiritual needs of my congregation, maintaining ties with families in the Middle East and across North America, and assisting the most vulnerable members of the parish had all taken a toll. Most likely, my high-stress lifestyle as leader of a fractious parish and confidant of the Metropolitan, as the archbishop of the church is called, had also played a role. At the time my health was becoming an issue, one of my most important projects had been the planning of a Celebration of Peace among the Jews, Muslims, and Christians of Montreal.[3] When I fell ill this time, the project was put on hold.

In early July of 2003, my mother, Nettie Sopp, the matriarch of the Gabriel family, passed away after a brief period of illness. Surgery for the persistent diverticulitis that had caused me such distress had been scheduled for early July. Of course, it was postponed for the funeral of our beloved mother.

By mid-July, my doctors had decided that a consultation with Dr. Barry Stein, a colorectal surgeon at the Montreal General Hospital, was necessary. My doctors were Dr. Roger Tabah, a well-known Montreal surgeon and a distant relative through my grandparents, and Dr. Eddie Tabah, a leading cancer physician and the first in our community to achieve recognition for his dedication and professionalism. The doctors decided I needed surgery to explore the possibility of straightening out the internal *mess*, which had been causing so much pain and discomfort. I was reluctant to undergo more surgery after my first near-death experience.

I remember overhearing a mother, at whose daughter's wedding I was to officiate in September, say, "Oh, no! He won't be here for the wedding!" And, as it turned out, I wasn't.

Illness is the night-side of life, a more onerous citizenship.

Everyone who is born holds dual citizenship, in the kingdom of the well and in the kingdom of the sick. Although we all prefer to use only the good passport, sooner or later each of us is obliged, at least for a spell, to identify ourselves as citizens of that other place.

—Susan Sontag, *Illness as a Metaphor*

CHAPTER 1

SILENCE IN THE MIDST OF CHAOS

On July 24, the day before entering Montreal General Hospital for my surgery, things did not get off to a good start. I had been directed to spend the day resting and cleansing in quiet preparation. Church politics decided otherwise. My assistant priest had brought home a bishop from the Middle East, and I was obliged to spend the day with him, trying to solve his immigration problems rather than preparing for surgery. This did nothing to calm my sense of foreboding about the coming procedure.

My wife, Lynn, was furious that I had agreed to see him. We had married when she was nineteen and I was twenty. Both of us had been students at seminary. I had been attracted by her faith, great sense of humor, striking beauty, and quick intelligence. Since our wedding, she has worked in anti-poverty programs, hosted radio and television programs, written and produced plays, and has traveled to Libya and Damascus to interview Colonel Qaddafi and President Assad. Most of all, she has been a dedicated mother and my alter ego in the parish. She knows me better than I know myself. She knew how difficult it was for me to set boundaries, even in preparation for this important surgery.

The next day, I went to the hospital. When I woke up after undergoing the procedure, the surgeon Dr. Stein said to us, "That went quite well."

I gripped Lynn's hand. "This was easy! I want to walk down the hall."

All progress ended that evening, however, and went downhill from there. Later in the evening, an alert nurse noticed that my vital signs were failing, my blood pressure had dropped to a dangerous level, and I was sinking fast. I have since learned that the surgical repair had ruptured.

As I was losing consciousness, I felt myself to be both in and out of my body. The phrase, *God is a whirlwind*, floated in my subconscious, and I could feel myself swirling into a vortex as I was borne back into the operating theater.

Thus began a long week of daily surgeries to repair the damage and to save my life. Many complications arose and septicemia set in. My family was called to my bedside. The last thing I heard as I descended into darkness was, "The Gabriel gang is coming."

Lynn called my older brother Charles. He came immediately from his home in Syracuse, New York. We have always been close, and he has always looked out for me. He was with Lynn and my sons David and Mark, when Dr. Stein told them there was little more he could do. Dr. Stein had actually been checking his Blackberry when he gave them this news. This enraged my wife. "You are telling me my husband is dying, and you're fooling around with your Game Boy!"

He retorted, "I am being shown a new procedure from the University of Boston Hospital. It is one I have never performed before!"

Another life-saving surgery began to repair the ruptures. The medical personnel told my family it would take hours, and, astonishingly, this gave Lynn a burst of confidence because it meant they were taking extreme measures to keep me alive! In the meantime, my brother went outside in the middle of the night, shook his fist, and demanded that God pull me back from the brink. He pleaded, "You just took my mother. Now you want my brother? I insist that you send him back!"

Lynn had been in the parking lot weeping when she saw Dr. Tabah, who had rushed to the hospital to observe the surgery. He exclaimed repeatedly, "This cannot be. This just cannot be!"

I later learned there had been a heated family discussion about what to do. My eldest son, David, had argued against the procedure they proposed for this sixth surgery. He told them that we had talked and he had promised he would not allow them to connect me to lifesaving mechanical contraptions. I had indeed told David that I would prefer to die rather than be connected to any mechanical devices as part of my daily routine. Lynn said, "I know your dad. He will pull through this no matter how difficult his recovery might be."

Prior to the initial surgery, I had had a feeling that this was not going to be easy, but nothing prepared me for the fact that the doctors were unable to stem the internal damage resulting from the ruptured intestine. When I decided to go ahead with the surgery, I had put my confidence in the surgeons. I had felt hopeful. The day after the operation, I had been up walking through the halls. Yet in one moment, it had all collapsed like a house of cards. In a microsecond, my life had been altered forever.

All the world's great religions of antiquity deal with the question of life after death. I had personally given this little thought except when I had officiated at funerals, that is, until my own brush with terminal cancer.

No one has yet been able to explain what happened in those early morning hours. It seems that after the rupture, there was a kind of implosion of my internal organs. Every time the doctors tried to repair my colon, the connection was unsuccessful and caused more damage.

The last operation in a series to try to repair the damage was the most difficult, as the doctors had tried, in laymen's terms, to rearrange the internal organs. They performed a double lobectomy and gave me a colostomy and a loop ileostomy. They left the incision open, held by clamps and with a kind of plastic tent covering my open wounds. There I lay for six weeks in a medically induced coma with the contents of my abdomen completely exposed. I was on a respirator; every possible vein was pierced with needles to administer morphine and all the medications I needed to stay alive.

There is a crack in everything
That's how the light gets in.

—Leonard Cohen. *Anthem.*

As I lay alone in this netherworld, I felt as if I was both in and out of my body. The phrase, *God is a whirlwind,*[4] again floated through my subconscious as I was swirling into a vortex. I think I was beginning to shed my body and enter into a new dimension where my *persona* or soul would be released to ascend to that uncreated light of divinity. I had a momentary taste of the peace that is beyond all earthly peace. In a brief flash, I saw myself swirling outside of my body.

For six weeks, I went in and out of that strange state. I heard familiar voices but could not understand them. I tried to make sense of where I was, who these people were, and what they were saying. During my silence, my subconscious will to live rose up. Lynn's voice was the most singular element that sustained me in this battle.

Scenes ebbed and flowed Walter-Mitty-like through my subconscious as I lay inert in the ICU. In one scene, the most glorious tree stood against a vivid blue sky at the end of a long tunnel. In my mind, I begged my wife to let me go to that tree. A magnetic force seemed to be tugging me towards it. When this scene appeared again to me, she was most insistent that I stay here. She turned me away from the tunnel. I heard her say, "Don't give up. You can't go there! Just hang on!"

In another scene, Lynn was on top of a hill. I climbed the hill to hear what she was saying to me. "Please. We are here. Hold on.

We love you!" she said. Then I rolled down the hill only to climb it again so I could ask her, "Why?" because I could not comprehend why she was telling me this.

The scenes constantly changed. In one moment, I was in a splendid, golden room where the clock on the wall had Roman numerals that were backward. Again, I wondered why. As the days rolled on, I was sure, at one point, I was in Ottawa at the governor-general's home attending a reception. In the next moment, I fled from this strange official occasion. I can still see myself, in my mind's eye, as the guest of the Prime Minister.

I constantly heard the chimes of bells of some kind that summoned me somewhere. In another scene, I lay on the ground at a gas station in Town of Mount Royal, wondering why I was there.

In one of the most terrifying scenes, I was in a prison. I thought I was Apollinaris of Posat, a Jesuit missionary who had been caught up in the French Revolution and tortured. His tormentors became my tormenters. They would approach my bed as I tried to fight them off. I thought I had surely fallen into the clutches of evil!

In another episode, a fox chased me as I screamed, "I want to live. I want to live!" Lynn's words hovered around me as I lay in this uneasy state of half being. "Don't let go. We are all here, and we love you!" she repeated.

To keep me stimulated and because of my interest in Middle Eastern politics, my brother-in-law Richard Rossy would read the Montreal Gazette's account of the war in Iraq to me. He would come into my room with the newspaper and say, "Hi, Kenny [my name

before ordination to the priesthood]. I am out here. Listen to this!"
However, in my mind I was in a Beirut jail! I could see my hands on
the bars and hear his voice outside. I wanted out!

In one brief waking moment, I saw a Spanish orderly, along
with others, beside my bed. They were all dressed in black. I was
convinced, as I slipped back under, that I was being pursued by the
devil. It turned out that they were Muslim nurses. Later, I chastised
them for wearing black in the ICU. "White! You should wear white!
Don't you realize that the patient has some level of awareness and
the sight of black is frightening?" I yelled.

I heard all sorts of voices and whispers. Some were inside
and some appeared to come from outside of my head. Some were
recognizable, but others were not. I tried hard to grasp their
meanings but could not. Many physicians from the parish came by
my room. They were shocked by what had happened, but I was not
really fully aware of their presence.

After the ordeal, Lynn and the others told me that I had been
quite a sight. My body had been pierced with needles and other
mechanisms to keep me alive. Because I had had chemotherapy
nearly ten years earlier, my veins were damaged. Intravenous
feeding, therefore, was done through and between my toes.

From time to time, the staff attempted to wake me up. Then for
a few moments, I recognized my brother Charles, my little sister
Sharon, and of course, Lynn. However, I only rarely glimpsed the
world outside, for I was in a shell and a state of suspended animation.

It was not long before I contracted MRSA (methicillin-resistant

Staphylococcus aureus), a staph infection that commonly lurks in hospital settings where patients may have open wounds and weakened immune systems. My situation immediately became more complicated. After six weeks in the ICU, I had to be transferred to a private room in isolation because of the MSRA.

Two young doctors from our parish were asked to stimulate my awakening after the move. The doctors took me up to a room on the eighteenth floor, which became my home for four months. As they wheeled my bed into the room, I could hear them shouting at me to get my attention, "*Abouna* [Father]! Do you know who we are? Are you waking up?"

Strangely enough, I gradually awoke with the words *God is a whirlwind* in the forefront of my mind—the last conscious thought I had had before going under. My brother and Lynn were in the room when the doctors wheeled me in.

I began to cry. "What happened to me?" I could hardly speak because of the respirator that had been down my throat for six weeks. All I could do was whisper.

Charles said, "Brother, I brought you back!" (He was referring to his challenge to God in the parking lot during the last surgery). Charles was convinced his prayerful plea had brought me back. It was Charles who later went to St. George Church to explain the situation to the hushed congregation, and he maintained communication with the archbishop.

My younger son, Mark, also arrived. He had left his work in Florida. Now he was literally on guard duty. He didn't allow calls or visits. I could see people, who were trying to get into the room, saying, "But we are close relatives!", while I was in isolation with my incision held together by the most painful clamps one could imagine. The only visitors my son allowed inside were my immediate family members. The children and grandchildren could only spend a few seconds with me.

Our daughter Tamara, who was Mark's twin, had been estranged from us after her nine-year-old daughter had been killed in an automobile accident. She called Lynn when she had heard the news to ask if she could see me.

When she came to visit me in the hospital, she brought me a new CD player so I could listen to music to soothe my restless spirit. Oleksa Lozowchuk, who had been a parishioner at the time, had composed a piece called "Bright Sadness." I remember hearing this beautiful music.

Mark asked my former cancer psychiatrist, Dr. John Pecknold, my lifeline during my first surgery in 1995, to help me cope with this new situation. Dr. Pecknold agreed to visit me. He met with a patient who could not comprehend what had happened to him.

Later, Dr. Tabah, my distant cousin who had originally proposed the surgery, came to my room. My immediate family members lived in Syracuse so they did not know much about my Montreal relatives, part of my large extended family. My brother Charles tried to block his entrance. Dr. Tabah came in crying, "Antony, how did this happen? Why did you do this to me? You came as close to dying as anyone I have ever seen in my medical profession."

We all wept together. It was hard for me to fathom. I did not learn until later that he and Lynn had met in the parking lot and had wept together, not knowing whether I would survive yet another operation.

The doctors and nurses tried to explain to me about the colostomy[5] and ileostomy[6], but it was beyond my understanding. I had so many tubes, needles, and devices in so many parts of my body, I did not even know exactly where *I* was. Because of all the antibiotics and fluids flowing into my body, I was constantly in a twilight zone. I did not know which side of the room I was on or whether I was right side up or upside down. It was a purgatory of suspended existence. Months afterward, I read the final, massive medical report, which indicated how many times resuscitation and surgical procedures were required. I finally grasped that my survival was both a mystery and a miracle.

There was a Greek church in Chicago where we once lived, and, for some reason, I imagined that I was seeing it from the window of my hospital room. However, I was on the eighteenth floor and there was no church in sight. I also saw something on the wall in my room from which I thought chimes were ringing. So many scenes swirled in and out of my semi-consciousness. I still felt isolated and alone in an abyss of pain and suffering.

One nurse named Sharon was unforgettably and unbelievably compassionate. I remember I was in my room; the doctors wanted more CT scans so they could investigate the nature of the infection that held me prisoner. Nurse Sharon stood up for me and said, "You must leave him alone!"

Later, a doctor came from the Infectious Disease Department and recommended yet another CT scan plus a new antibiotic, Vancomycin. My wife wrote, faxed, and begged the doctors, "Please, no more antibiotics! I know my husband! He's fighting and will get through this without any further assaults on his already fragile system."

Sharon, my youngest sibling and only sister, and Lynn continued their efforts to prevent the doctors from prescribing antibiotics. Then a new doctor wrote an order for a drug for a scan. It was difficult for my body to accept the dye in this drug. Instinctively I knew I would pay for this intrusion.

Sure enough, a week after I had been transferred from the ICU, I went into acute renal failure. My body was bloated, and skin was falling off my hands and feet (To this day, they are quite sensitive, as I suffer from neuropathy). Again I was rushed into surgery to have a catheter inserted in my jugular vein so dialysis could begin at once, and again Lynn was called in the middle of the night to come and give her permission for the procedure. My body was shutting down, and I needed help immediately.

The nephrologist on duty later said, "This man was so close to death it is a miracle he is still alive!"

I spent that same night sitting in a chair, unable to move, the dialysis machine attached to my neck.

One complication followed another. A Lebanese nurse drove me crazy during my first days in dialysis. She pretended she did not recognize me even though I had helped her husband get his first job when they had immigrated to Canada. She peppered me with very unwelcome questions about suicide, which, at that very moment, seemed a plausible solution to my situation.

Three days a week, they wheeled my bed to the dialysis unit. Again, I had trouble piecing the story together—the big *why*? Why had my kidneys betrayed me? I pleaded with the nephrology team to jump-start my kidneys, but they were unable to do so. I cried silently at this latest turn of events.

They called Lynn to the hospital every night during those weeks because they feared I was slipping away. Lynn, Sharon, Charles, our close friends Cookie and Larry Rossy and the children lived in a state of constant vigil, never knowing what crisis would come next.

In the end, I spent four months at the hospital in a dreamlike state, and in almost total silence. It was during this of all times that my book *Gabriel's Dragon*, which described my 1995 battle with metastatic colon cancer, was published. It lay unopened on the stand next to my bed. I never even picked it up, so utterly disinterested was I in the minutiae of daily activities.

My older brother Charles often came from Syracuse to support Lynn and me. While he was staying at our home, he often spoke to the congregation at our church to quiet their concerns. He also fielded calls that poured in from people from all walks of life who wanted to know about my health. The Prime Minister of Canada, the Premier of Quebec, the Mayor of Montreal, the Cardinal Archbishop, and many prominent politicians from all levels called. At one point while I was in isolation, he turned to me and said,

"Who in the hell are you?" I guess he was surprised that his little brother moved in such a range of circles.

I continued to exist in a state of restlessness even while remaining in a silent fog. From time to time, I would question Lynn. "Do we have a home? Children? A car?" To each she replied "Yes!" To jolt me to reality, she said, "Even the dog misses you."

"Dog!" I shouted. "We don't have a dog!" Then she knew I was coming back.

She had plastered the walls of my room with pictures, children's drawings, get well cards, and a huge calendar that marked the days I was in the hospital. I looked at them, but it would be a long time before I would really see what they were.

Lynn was the positive force that kept me moving forward. She and Tammy brought a fan to keep me cool during those hot summer days. They also cleaned the room every day. Although I was very fortunate to have a private room, the living conditions were far from ideal. Budget cutbacks and labor union rules meant that the cleanliness of the room left a great deal to be desired.

However, it was the colostomy and ileostomy appliances—the bags to collect feces—that were the most difficult to deal with. I could almost accept the radical surgery - but not the appliances! On top of everything else, my kidney failure threw me into a deep depression. I pleaded with the doctors. "Why? You must do something. This is unacceptable!" The three days a week I spent in dialysis connected through my jugular vein were a heavy burden, and managing the appliances was almost too much to bear.

One of my nurses was Spanish. She collected my blood each day. Once, I noticed a vial around her neck. "What is in the little tube?" I asked.

"Your blood. The blood of a priest is like the blood of Christ."

Ugh, I thought. She had difficulty drawing blood each day and even had to use my feet. It was so painful. There was no part of my body that did not ache. Then there was the catheter in my neck for the dialysis. What position could I assume to be even a bit comfortable?

The noise and chaos in the hospital nearly drove me mad. I was completely disoriented. Because of the incessant beeping and lights on at all hours of the day and night, the room seemed to be in a perpetual state of change. Was another person there with me? I was sure someone was patting my left arm, that my dead mother was telling me that all was going to be okay... Where was the real me?

Two psychiatrists came to see me in response to concerns voiced by the nurses. Trying to assess my mental state, I suppose, they asked me if I thought someone was present in the room. I responded sheepishly, "Yes!" I felt the presence of my newly departed mother tapping me on my upper arm as she often did when I visited her at home.

Blood tests ordered by the two psychiatrists revealed that my thyroid had shut down. This may have contributed to my absolute lethargy.

To help me gain mobility, the nurses slid me from my bed to a chair called the "McGill Chair". At first, I sat up for fifteen minutes.

Each day they increased my sitting time. After that, they got me walking, little by little. I had to relearn how to walk, climb steps… Remember, I had not walked in months.

I hardly knew where to begin. They sent teams of physical therapists and colostomy nurses in to teach me how to return to regular, daily life. In addition, they turned me every four hours to prevent bedsores.

Someone brought me a mirror so I could look at myself. I almost fainted when I saw the insides of my abdomen which had been left open so I could heal from the inside out. Dr. Stein told me, "The body is a marvel in the way it can recover from extreme trauma and heal itself." After three months, they finally removed the clamps. Each change was liberation.

I remember when I first really woke up, I asked for water. The nurse brought me a jug. Suddenly, the head nurse rushed in. She had realized immediately that this had been a mistake. They had only allowed me to have a few ice chips at a time. She rushed in to retrieve the jug. Before she reached me, I took it and dumped the water all over myself. I had not bathed in months.

She exclaimed, "Alleluia! The priest has baptized himself!"

I have set before you life and death, blessing and cursing: therefore choose life.

—Deuteronomy 30:19 (KJV)

CHAPTER 2

INTO THE LIGHT

My next challenge was to learn how to care for my various appliances, including the catheter in my jugular vein for dialysis. This was difficult because my belly was still full of stitches and tubes.

I told my nurses, Christian and Sharon, "The whole time I spent in a coma I was fighting a battle between good and evil." I honestly believed this and tried to come to terms with how I should move forward.

It was the job of my nurses, Christian and Elaine, to teach me how to use my colostomy and ileostomy appliances and to clean myself. I resisted. One day Elaine came in and saw my book, *Gabriel's Dragons*.

"Did you write this?" she asked.

"Yes," I said weakly as she turned the pages and found a passage that referred to courage in adversity.

She quipped, "Courage? Are you a big hypocrite?" She went on,

"I am going to sit on you until *you* take care of the colostomy and ileostomy. You need to begin the road to independence." She made me understand that I had no choice; I had to do this. It was the one thing I dreaded most besides dialysis.

So the long journey began, first to deal with the appliance and then to sit in the McGill Chair and later, to take baby steps with a walker and, eventually, walk, using a cane. I still could not speak above a whisper.

A daily procession of surgeons, psychiatrists, endocrinologists, hematologists, physical therapists and nephrologists arrived, with an army of assistants and students coming and going at a dizzying pace. I was constantly being poked, probed and questioned. That is the downside of being a patient in a teaching hospital.

A procession of doctors came in just to see me. Some said, "We just wanted to see who you really are!" Another told me, "The medical staff has given strict orders: 'Save this man or else!'"

The head of our church at that time, Archbishop Philip Saliba, frequently phoned our home and issued an order that no visitors or phone calls be allowed in my room. It was much later that a few people were permitted for a few minutes and only those who had known me for years as their pastor.

One exception was an old friend, Bishop Joseph Al-Zehlaoui, now the Archbishop, who was in Montreal from Los Angeles. He came to see me for a few quiet moments. Unable to fake it, I choked up when I saw him.

Another bishop, George Abou Zahkem, had come from

Damascus to attend a wedding at which I was supposed to officiate. He was an old and dear friend, but I would not allow him to come in because I was still hallucinating. From the corner of my eye, I could see that he wore his black robes. Just before his arrival, I had watched a report on CNN about the spread of the West Nile virus. When he came into my room, he was transformed in my mind's eye into a big, black insect. It was several years before I could explain this to him.

As I returned to life on this planet, Lynn allowed a few family visitors, which included my nephews, the clergy assistants from the church, and my office staff. In this way, outside events began to intrude into my silent space. The real world had found me. My secretary and the parish psychologist brought me details of a crisis that had erupted in the parish, with everyone taking sides, as was usually the case with such matters. This nearly pushed me over the edge.

My son Mark had offered to stay with me and to help by working with the children in the parish. Everyone loved Mark, who is very kind and giving and has a wicked sense of humor. Some powerful laymen, however, vetoed this generous offer, apparently believing that having a father and a son working together was not a good idea. I was too fragile to put up much of a fight. I think they believed I would not survive the latest crisis. This was another setback.

Sometimes while I was undergoing dialysis alone, Lynn allowed a few friends to see me. They helped to whittle away the hours. Many wept when they saw my condition, crying in Arabic, "O gracious St. George. O Holy Mary! How could you allow this to happen?"

My world mainly consisted of the hospital staff. Infrequently, someone would visit from Lebanon or Syria and would insist on seeing me. These friends had lived in Montreal during the unrest in the Middle East. They brought news from the outside world as I underwent dialysis. While it was upsetting in some ways, especially to the nursing staff, at least I felt somewhat connected to the outside world.

Lynn was the one who knew that I would pull through. She called in some pastoral counselors but allowed very few clergy visits. She wanted me to fight and not to be spooked by a stream of black-robed priests reciting ritualistic prayers over me. She also needed to keep the curious at bay, even though there was a "No Visitors" sign on the door. Some members of the clergy even called my brother at home to ask for a cross or some object to remember me by! Lynn's vigilance protected me from these invasions.

While I was surrounded by kindness, I also experienced some bizarre, disturbing, and unprofessional behavior from some of the medical personnel. One nurse demanded I give her a daily kiss. A male nurse would poke, probe, and then pray over me. A multitude of doctors, especially the female ones, literally cried each time I had to have a new procedure. Most of the nurses were unbelievably kind. However, most said, as did the physicians, they had never known a patient who had endured so much physical trauma. They were in awe of how I survived each calamity.

When I was informed that I had suffered acute kidney failure, I had remained in a state of utter disbelief. I begged the nephrologist, Dr. Murray Vasilevsky, to say it was not so. As he held my hand and with tears in his eyes, Dr. Vasilevsky said, "I will do everything in my power to see you through this." No matter how many times I questioned how this could have happened, he had no answers. He could not tell me when I would be free of the dialysis.

I did not know if I would ever reach the bottom of this black hole of despair into which I had sunk. I was no longer sure I would be able to climb out of it, either. No matter how they tried to explain the events of the previous months, I could not assimilate the knowledge that something so dramatic had happened to me without anyone really knowing how or why!

The terror I had at night was the worst. It was awful. I relived all that had happened to me. All the scenes that had unfolded in the silence of my coma, now drifted in and out of my subconscious as I pondered my own life experiences, good and bad, over the past sixty-five years. I still get shivers when I remember many of the scenes that had flitted through my head when I was in a coma. I would remember the strange stream of subconscious, random thoughts; the altered states of emotion, the struggles, and the memories I had inhabited, perhaps because of all the medications and painkillers I was on. Images floated incessantly and disturbingly around in my head. In my state of semi-awareness, some of these dream-like visions were like a long nightmare. At times, I awoke, grasping at reality only to have it slip away. Sound and images flowed randomly only to disappear into oblivion. The frustration!

Sleep eluded me. CNN became my companion in the evenings, although most of the news was still incomprehensible to me. It was a sound I could cling to. As I became able to absorb the news,

I realized it was not good; the conflict in the Middle East seemed likely to go on for years.

When dawn would finally appear after another restless night, I would anxiously wait for my surgeon, Dr. Stein, or the nephrologist, Dr. Vasilevsky. They were my lifelines of hope for leaving the hospital. Though I constantly peppered them and their aides with questions, I understood little while I remained in this foggy state of being.

I had never heard of *creatine* or *creatinine*[7] and was unable to process the information the staff tried to give me. The thought of renal failure on top of everything else was too much to bear. My fear of the future was so pervasive I became frozen. Never having had kidney problems before, I experienced renal failure as a deep personal failure. Would my life ever be normal again? Would I ever regain my independence? No one had an answer for me. We were in unknown territory.

Later, as my independence grew little by little, I gradually took a few tentative steps outside the hospital room. After a while, Lynn and my mother-in-law, Janna, would force me to use a walker and slowly walk to the park on the hospital grounds. The first walk down the hallway, however, was my first walking victory. Later, I graduated to a cane until I could maneuver under my own steam.

One day, I pleaded with my son Mark to drive me home so I could see the house. It was another tentative step toward extricating myself from the hospital.

On Thanksgiving, which occurs in early October in Canada,

I begged the staff to let me go to my sister's house for lunch. Mark offered to drive me, and I would only stay for an hour or so. I could not eat lunch there because of my strict renal diet. However, it was a victory for the hospital staff, who cared so much about me, that I wanted to take such a step. They even had a little cake to celebrate.

The days of October passed and my rehabilitation continued, interspersed with dialysis sessions. On Halloween, news came that I would be released from the hospital. The first plan was to have me go to a convalescent home. However, Dr. Stein ruled that out. Instead, he extended my stay at the hospital so he could keep a watchful eye on my progress prior to sending me home. Thank God for this small mercy. I could not even contemplate going from the hospital to a convalescent home. I wanted to go *home*.

At last, the day came! My mother-in-law had prepared a celebration supper and had brought some friends to help. Everyone was there to greet me and to welcome me back home. They were in the kitchen laughing and drinking wine and chatting. I sat on a stool by myself, looking at this group as if they were from another planet—or maybe I was. After four months of virtual silence, the social clamor got to me. I became completely disoriented and very upset. I was not ready for social interaction.

Finally, I climbed down from my stool and crawled upstairs. I ripped off my clothes and looked at myself in our bathroom mirror. I saw my skinny body, a catheter in my neck, my hated colostomy and ileostomy appliances and my sticklike legs and had a complete meltdown. I wept like a baby. My temperature rose so high that

Lynn called the doctor who ordered me to be taken by ambulance to back to the hospital's ICU.

This was not the first time I had to be taken to the hospital by ambulance or carried into the emergency room or ICU unit that fall and winter. Never will I forget one trip to the ER. I went by ambulance with Lynn. Finally, about midnight, the doctors sent her home. I remained in the hallway where an elderly man was snoring so loudly I wanted to crawl out of my skin. Nobody would listen to my plea that I had had MSRA and had two appliances that needed care, or that I had been a patient in that very hospital. I remained there until Lynn came the next morning at six o'clock to take me back home.

Often when I checked into the nephrology unit before leaving the hospital, I had to undergo blood transfusions because my hemoglobin was so low. I felt that I was never going to be free of these visits, which occurred so frequently for the first six months after leaving the hospital.

How do I describe being *home*? How many times did I fall down the steps? The skin on my hands and feet cracked open due to renal failure. I had to wear white gloves to prevent infection. My diet was extremely restrictive. The CLSC, the local community health center that should have liaised with my hospital caregivers, was, for all intents and purposes, invisible. We didn't even know that home care nurses were available. Lynn had to manage me by herself. She kept me clean and tracked all my medications—blood supplements, prednisone, pain, sleep, thyroid pills, and so on. What a nightmare!

A man named Peter came to stay with us, supposedly to help us.

My mother-in-law had suggested he come, as a way of helping him and me. He had left his wife and son in Holland and had fled to the United States. Then he had sneaked into Canada for safety. He was using us as a cover, which we did not know. He did help, but I found his heavy, brooding presence in my home upsetting.

I could not sleep. I constantly itched, had cracked skin on my extremities, and sores all over my body. My hair fell out. When I walked, I felt like I was treading on broken glass. How many times did the colostomy or ileostomy bags fall off at night? I had not bathed for close to a year!

Three times a week, a cab would take me to the hospital for dialysis, which was an all-day affair. This went on until December. Would I ever escape from this awful netherworld?

I relapsed again, and they rushed me back to the ICU. The team of doctors came in and said, "We have to move the catheter in your neck and put it on the other side. It is badly infected." I looked at the doctors and said baldly, "No. I do not want to continue this charade. I have so many openings that when I drink I leak."

It seemed nothing was going to get my kidneys to work again. I was tired practically to death. I said, "Please, no more torture! Now I just want to let nature take its course and be allowed to go."

The doctors replied, "Please give us a chance. We know that you have been through a rough time. We will return in an hour after we study the options."

Meanwhile, I requested to see a priest. He and I were not on good terms. When he came, I asked that he bury the past and pray for me.

After he left, a Haitian nurse came in and said, "Did I hear you're giving up? For six weeks, you were in this bed dying, and we all worked hard to keep you living. We didn't do it. It was God! He has a mission for you. Do you hear me? Don't give up. You will betray God who still has use for you." To this day, I do not know who she was, hard as I have tried to find her. She gave me the push I needed, and I would have liked to thank her.

The doctors returned. They laid out their proposal. "We want you to take an experimental program of blood supplements, steroids, and blood power shots." This was an expensive cocktail of medication, which I would take for the next month. Then they would take me off dialysis. The shot alone cost one thousand dollars, the blood supplements were five hundred dollars, and the pills were one hundred dollars each.

Reluctantly, I agreed to this program of intense medical treatment, and it worked! My creatinine levels gradually descended enough that I would be able to stay off dialysis. This was another liberation!

Soon I received one more liberation—Peter was finally leaving. Lynn arranged for our close friends, who were also my little cousins, Dr. Tom Saba and his twin sister, Kathy, an oncology nurse, to stay with me while she took Peter back to the United States. I was very happy to see the last of him. And I will never forget Dr. Saba's and Kathy's tender, loving care. Myriam Sphortun, who is married to my former assistant, Father Peter, also came and stayed with me during this time.

It was still difficult for me to eat. My food tasted dreadful. All the medication plus the strict renal diet, which was not exciting in the least, had ruined my sense of taste. On top of the renal diet my new colon diet was another unwelcome test, even though Lynn worked very hard to find and prepare the proper food for my nourishment and pleasure. Occasionally, one of my close parishioner friends would bring a little supper and pass the evening with me, which brought me consolation. After many months of solitude and isolation, I relished the company of friends.

Other members of my church pitched in and offered help when I returned home. George Fattouch, the church's chanter, did reflexology on me to help my kidneys. One parishioner, Gene Beauchamp, brought me a treadmill so I could rebuild my leg muscles. Another parishioner, Larry Rossy, sent me a trainer, who gave me physical therapy for a month or so. I was not going to give up without a fight for survival and healing, and I had help. Our bedroom looked like a hospital room because of all the appliance materials and medications.

In the past, I had had difficulty coping with anger when dealing with trivial issues. However, staring death in the face made it imperative that I spend time in silence and prayer. Joyful suffering had to be enfleshed, to be given bodily form, made real, accepted into my very self so I could continue. When suffering comes as a gift, it becomes a mission of grace, which allows the recipient to touch others.

I would sit for hours in my study, which was filled with icons and my large library of scriptures and prayer books, and absorb the positive energy that emanated from these sources of spirituality.

Once I had been freed from the catheter in my jugular vein, I wanted to go to church to thank God for this deliverance. I was determined to go to the church one snowy Sunday morning in December of 2003 against all opposition and advice from the archbishop, my family, and all our friends. It was important that I do this so I could return to sanity and start down the road to recovery. In retrospect, it was probably foolish to venture out, yet I had felt compelled to do so from deep inside.

My brother-in-law Richard agreed to be my chauffeur. It was so important to thank everyone for his or her love and support. As I walked haltingly up the aisle, the parishioners cried, clapped, and blew me kisses because I could not have any physical contact with them. I stood at the altar with the help of my cane. It was a highly-charged moment. I remember telling the congregation, "Rid yourselves of anger and angst. Life is so short. Everything can change in a flash." I also thanked them fervently for their prayers.

In my heart of hearts, I believe I survived because of the prayers that were being said around the world. There were so many people praying that this spiritual energy sustained and surrounded my sinful person and elevated me to another dimension of being. I later learned that friends in Syria, Lebanon, the United States, Russia, and the Montreal community were saying prayers in liturgies and private assemblies.

For months on end, there was a kind of solemn silence at St.

George Church during the divine services. I believe that the energy of these supplications reached God and the depth of my soul. This was a sublime mystery, which could not be taken for granted or explained.

More things are wrought by prayer
than this world dreams of.

—Tennyson, The Passing of Arthur"

CHAPTER 3

PICKING UP THE PIECES

I have written about my ordeal, but the real hero was Lynn, my helpmeet. She endured, beyond all measure, the daily stress of not knowing what would happen or even what to expect. In the end, she was worn to a frazzle. I would not have survived if she had not been at my side. She dealt with the doctors and made sure that everything that could be done was done. When they did not heed her message regarding the antibiotics and drugs, I ended up with acute renal failure. Everyone has told me that Lynn and my sister were real heroines because of their passionate care and concern for me. They held everyone accountable.

The following spring, Lynn was diagnosed with kidney cancer and was told she required immediate surgery. Our son David and her cousin Dr. Mike Neam came for the operation. They told us it was a malignant tumor. After two weeks, they told her that it was not, in fact, a tumor. In the meantime, her incision herniated, and she was in absolute agony. She had contacted C. difficile[8], and had just recovered from it. Another bout could have been fatal given her condition. Her body was exhausted and fragile from directing all her strength and energy to me.

Who took care of whom? Now, it was almost laughable. There were two surgical patients under one roof. The doctor from St. Mary's Hospital who did her surgery accepted no responsibility for the hernia. In the end and after suffering so much pain, Lynn went to a clinic in Maryland that specializes in surgical hernias to repair the damage.

The day she came home after her surgery was Monday of Holy Week in the Orthodox church. Holy Week proceeded at a dizzying pace. I was up early since sleep evaded me that year after my surgery. I exercised on the treadmill and cared for my appliances. I then brought Lynn home from the hospital and ran to church. Then I returned home to check on her and went back to church for the evening Holy Week Service of the Bridegroom.

Tuesday was the same routine except that I also went to McGill University where I had been teaching for years. Then I returned home to check on Lynn and ran back to the church.

Wednesday was the same, plus a funeral. After, I went home to check on Lynn and to deal with my appliances before returning to church for the Holy Wednesday Anointing of Healing Service. This is a special service in the Orthodox church, which includes the ceremony of the washing of the feet. Then I went back home to settle Lynn in for the night.

Holy Thursday, I went through my usual morning routine then went to an early morning liturgy of the Lord's Supper, followed by yet another funeral. I returned to the church after going to the cemetery and to another funeral. Then I went back home to check on Lynn, to look after my appliances, and go to McGill. I then went back to church for the Holy Thursday Twelve Passion Gospels' Service.

Holy Friday, more of the same. Then, a terrible personal blow fell when a young and dynamic member of the parish, John Rossy [9] suddenly died. I visited his family, a difficult visit, and then went back and forth between the church and the house.

By the time Easter arrived, I wondered if I was having a nervous breakdown. Our services could be quite long and the appliances were always a concern lest they fall off during church. In addition, my mind was never far from Lynn.

On the weekend, Lynn's mother and her friend Bob arrived for Easter. When Lynn tried to get out of bed, she fell down the bed's steps and gashed her head on the tile floor. I thought she was dead because there was blood everywhere. I immediately called for an ambulance, which arrived almost immediately. We spent the night at the Montreal General Hospital ER, where she received stitches and was released. When I called for the ambulance, lo and behold, the police showed up to ensure her injury was not due to domestic violence.

I could not help but think of the endless challenges that kept coming our way. I nevertheless realized God had kept me around for a reason. What followed in the life of our church community validated this. For example, we brought an orphan boy from Lebanon to a couple in our congregation, fulfilling their dream of having a child. The boy had been left on the steps of the police station in the outskirts of Beirut. Our mission during this uncivil war in Lebanon was to bring twenty children to Canada to be adopted by families in the parish.

All this uncertainty and worry led me away from my old self. It is difficult to put on paper what took place inside my heart during this period. I became more reflective. As far as my family members were concerned, I craved their presence and appreciated them as never before. I now knew how fragile life was and that every minute must be a prayerful celebration. I felt born anew by the grace of God like a butterfly as it emerges from its cocoon.

Meanwhile, Lynn bore everything that happened and managed to maintain her equilibrium and care for others, although she continued to suffer from her surgery. Then to make matters worse, while she was on her way to see her naturopath near Sherbrooke, a thug beat her up in a road rage incident. When he attacked her, he re-injured the operation site. Lynn had to later return to the Maryland clinic for more surgery, and to this day, she suffers psychologically and physically from this incident.

In the end, we realized our only choice was to push ourselves through each moment, knowing that God was with us. No one else knew the depth of suffering we were going through. We tried to keep up a brave face. God was there. We found Him in the silence of internal prayer. Reading the Bible as a method of meditation helped us let Him work in His own way and gave us courage and strength during our darkest hours.

Once I was freed from the ordeal of dialysis, I began a semi-normal existence but still had to deal with the appliances. I spent many days in the ostomy clinic so they could help me maintain the bags. It was a kind of humiliation that was difficult to live with and it was extremely limiting. Going to the clinic made me feel so dependent on others. Each time I went to the floor where I had spent four months, I got the shivers.

The daily swim, which had been so much a part of my life, had to be abandoned. Instead, I used the treadmill at home to rebuild my strength. I needed a walking stick because I was still wobbly. Everything hurt. I felt like an old man as I tried to maneuver and carry out my daily chores.

During the first year after my surgery, I could not sleep. I tried everything. At least seeing psychiatrist Dr. John Pecknold helped me deal with the mental stress of the trauma I had undergone and to adjust to this new life.

I also began to make limited parish visits. On one such occasion, a former parishioner who had married a Jewish businessman wanted me to visit her. Her cousin picked me up, and off we went to their exquisite Westmount home. During the lavish supper, I felt my bag slipping. I excused myself from the table and went to the washroom. When I tried to check it, the bag flew out from my pants and splattered on her expensive wallpaper. I was tearfully trying to clean up the mess when the parishioner rapped on the door and said, "I know what happened. It happened to my aunt. Open up so we can help." After that experience, I planned my public forays carefully and limited them.

I also had to get back to the church to make sure things were running smoothly, because they were not. The priest and the deacon did not understand one another. They were from two different cultures, so there were constant clashes. There was a multitude of other problems, including financial problems, and I had to use all my energy to pull the parish together. My absence had allowed some major fissures to erupt that required healing. "My God," I cried, "I cannot even be ill in peace without unleashing a series of calamities! I cannot be everywhere at once!"

Lynn had taken over my course on Eastern Mysticism and Contemporary Literature at McGill. I would appear from time to time, but she became the main lecturer with some assistance from specialists in various mystical trends—Christian, Islamic, and Jewish. Dr. Issa Boulatta, Michel Naggiar. Some of the students who had a special interest in the Kabala or Sufism assisted her. Then, after her operation for what we believed was kidney cancer, I returned to finish teaching the course.

My limited participation caught the attention of the government tax department. I was receiving disability payments at the time. The government bureaucrats insisted that I was not disabled. They expected that I would be totally immobilized! They came after us for the small pittance that the university paid us!

Dealing with insurance and health care bureaucracies— Revenu Québec, Revenue Canada (the taxation arm of the federal and provincial governments), the Régie de l'assurance maladie (the Quebec government health insurance agency), and the disability program under the Quebec pension plan—was really the final straw. I still have boxes of correspondence from this difficult time.

As our bills mounted, I was obliged to fight on many fronts. Taxes, bills, and correspondence with both Revenue Canada and Revenu Québec! It was all too much for me. It went on nonstop, like Chinese water torture on my forehead. I felt completely at the mercy of the government and the bureaucrats, who cared little about an ailing person. They just wanted their pound of flesh. It was enough to make one pull one's hair out. It was a kind of purgatory! I felt I was being punished for living. This could be the subject of another book!

During my convalescence, the late archbishop, Philip Saliba, who had bestowed on me the title of Economos (an honorific used for married priests), requested that I prepare a chancery for the new bishop who would be coming to serve in the newly established Diocese of Ottawa Eastern Canada and upstate New York. This was another challenge.

Montreal was chosen because the new bishop, Alexander Mufarrij, insisted on coming to this city rather than to Ottawa. One reason was the large Orthodox Christian population in Montreal and another was that he wanted to live in a metropolitan city.

It would take me an entire book to describe the politics, personalities, demands, and hard work that I would need to pull this off. Ottawa wanted him there. Everyone had a different opinion as to the location of the new chancery.

The Church of St. Mary's in Montreal, which was born out of St.

George and had a large population of immigrants (described in my book, *Gabriel's' Dragon*), owned a suitable house that was empty. Its pastor was ambivalent about our using it. However, the large property of the church's site would be subject to taxes if this presbytery, earlier leased by nuns, was not used as a rectory or chancery.

It took long hours, much stress, and the intervention of Bishop Antoun Khoury, who was the auxiliary to the archbishop and the late Ernest Saykaly, to help the clergy and the laity of the new diocese negotiate a solution and put all dissensions to bed so the large building could be suitably renovated for the new bishop.

When I look back at this period, I honestly have no idea what kept me going. The winter and spring of 2004 was a constant challenge, compounded by Lynn's health scare. I had to stay mentally positive if I wanted to survive all these challenges.

I had no alternative but to fight. I was going to fight hard, especially to rid myself of the hated appliances. Every night I went to my study and worked on my spirituality, calling on all the powers above to push me toward mental and physical wellness. In fact, this became my main job. I wanted the colostomy and ileostomy reversed. That decision required military-strength and mental training to reorient my whole existence. Anyone who has these appliances knows how they can change a person's routine and affect his or her whole life.

To do this, I needed to make my kidneys stronger and get my body in shape. Every visit to Dr. Stein, the ostomy clinic, or the nephrology department dealt solely with the necessary steps to rebuild my *broken machine*. I always left them feeling disheartened.

The doctors tried their best to encourage me about my progress, which was miraculous to them but not to me. I still lived in a world of unacceptable subservience to the body that had betrayed me and the humiliation of having to deal with the appliances.

At times, I was frustrated while going for check-ups by my nephrologist Dr. Vasilevsky since I often required blood transfusions, which took up a large part of the day. However, I owe my surgeons, Dr. Stein and Dr. Vasilevsky and nurse Marie Lecavalier a huge debt of gratitude. They never gave up. I believe they saved my life. In the end, they gave me courage to fight on.

They pointed heavenward whenever I praised them. They truly felt as though the hand of God had pulled me through. They had no scientific reason for thinking otherwise. My emotions, at that time, were so ambivalent. I felt hope, despair, and then hope again.

Occasionally, I was asked to speak to a class at McGill about my experiences. The students in my religion class were intensely interested in these stories. I also lectured about my close brush with death to groups outside of the church and received the benefits of talking about the ordeal and sharing with others. Because I was a cancer survivor and had also lost a grandchild, I counseled patients and families—something that I do to this day.

Helping others is a kind of reverse energy. One gives, and the gift returns in kind. Reaching out to and trying to help others really forced me to transcend my own little world and my pain. To be a wounded healer and to be able to touch others with a moment of grace is a real gift that comes only from God, who is the ultimate source of all grace and power.

Your pain is the breaking of the shell that encloses your understanding.

Even as the stone of the fruit must break ... so must you know pain.

And could you keep your heart in wonder at the daily miracles of your life, your pain would not seem less wondrous than your joy;

And you would accept the seasons of your heart ....

And you would watch with serenity through the winters of your grief.

—Khalil Gibran, *on Pain in The Prophet.*

CHAPTER 4

COMING TO TERMS

What time I could spare for my own health concerns after juggling these various crises, I spent preparing to return to a normal life without the hated appliances. For this I would need an operation to reconnect my colon. The hospitals in Montreal were not ready to do what I wanted. The surgeons here do colon repair in several stages, and I wanted to do the procedures in one operation. *C. difficile* was rampant in Montreal hospitals at that time. I knew I could never survive another situation like the one I had just passed through.

I spoke to Barry Stein, a Montreal lawyer, who was the chairman of the Colorectal Foundation. He had gone to New York for a similar procedure; the doctors had closed the opening in his colon so he could be rid of the appliances. I asked him what he advised. His answer was, "You should look at the Mayo Clinic." This was what my family wanted as well.

Lynn and my family researched Mayo Clinic facilities and hospitals in other cities for the surgery. My son, David, a fellow at the Mayo Clinic in Rochester, suggested various possibilities. We finally settled on the Mayo Clinic in Scottsdale, Arizona, where we had once lived and still had many friends, some of whom are even distant relatives. I had known others since 1962, when I had gone there to be the pastor of my first church.

We contacted surgeon Dr. Jacques Heppell, who had an outstanding reputation. We asked other physicians, who knew him from Montreal's Hôtel-Dieu Hospital where he had practiced colorectal surgery, about him. Dr. Heppell had moved to the United States to practice because he had felt that the Quebec health care bureaucracy did not allow him to perform the challenging surgeries he wanted and was trained to do.

In June of 2004, we finally made an appointment to see him. He quickly agreed to see me. Of course, my physician in Montreal also contacted him.

Lynn was adamant that this was the only route. Every time I brought up the financial aspect of it, she retorted, "Debt or death!" Lynn worked the internet thoroughly and was convinced that there was no other alternative. She took my care in hand and became, as she had been called during my hospital stay when she had refused admission to parishioners, my "health Nazi."

I gave a few more lectures before we left for Arizona. The last one was an evening sponsored by the Cedars Cancer Fund, which was supported by the Montreal Lebanese community and the Royal Victoria Hospital, where I spoke to cancer patients.

The evening was dedicated to cancer patients and survivors.

The topic was what one had to do to battle metastatic cancer. I was on a panel chaired by Dr. Roger Tabah and Gwen Nacos of Cancer Support. I told my story and spoke of my experience. As I was speaking, my appliance was sliding off and gradually slipping down my pants. I finished quickly and literally bolted out of the room without saying goodbye. That was it! I was going to the Mayo! I wanted no more of this. I called Lynn and asked her to please make the final arrangements.

Persistence paid off. Dr. Stein had sent Dr. Heppell all the reports. Dr. Heppell was ready to receive us. I went to the Montreal General Hospital's ostomy clinic to be "wrapped" to protect my appliances for the plane ride to Arizona. Our dear friends Sally and David Ghiz, whom we have known for fifty years, arranged to meet us and they looked after all our living arrangements while were in Phoenix. David's father, George, was a good friend with whom I had worked at the archdiocese for many years after leaving Phoenix, and so was his wife Sally. David was a youngster when I was in Phoenix, but somehow, we never lost our connection, which had deepened over the years on other trips to Arizona.

Lynn made the flight arrangements, including asking for a wheelchair, since I was still quite frail. We left Montreal with both trepidation and anxiety. What would this trip accomplish? Would Dr. Heppell be able to do both closures in one surgical procedure?

David Ghiz greeted us at the Phoenix airport and took us directly to the Phoenician, one of the best resorts in North America. Another instance of synchronicity: to return to the same place where I had begun my priestly ministry in 1962!

The next day we were up early and Sally drove us to my first appointment before seeing Dr. Heppell. After examining me, the nephrologist said, "Put a dollar in the collection plate. You have done amazingly well. I believe you can do this surgery without any further problems with your kidneys." Another Rubicon crossed.

David joined us. We ran into a businessman he knew, who had been healed in an extraordinary manner by Dr. Heppell.

When I walked into Dr. Heppell's examining room, the former Quebecker shook my hand warmly and said, "Bonjour!" We spoke a bit in French. His intense expression and serious manner gave me confidence. A sixth sense told me instantly he was the man I wanted for my surgery. After reading my reports and examining me, he said, "A double closure would be dangerous for you, and I am not sure I can do it successfully, considering the complications." (He meant my delicate kidneys).

He went on to give me a clear appraisal of the risks of surgery in cases such as mine. He concluded, "There is a fifty-fifty survival rate.". Nothing, however, could make me waver. I wanted him to do this. It was his modesty and humble confidence that reassured both Lynn and me.

The surgery was set for June 24, the Feast of St. John the Baptist, a Quebec holiday that celebrates Quebecois society and culture.[10] The week before my surgery, I decided to build up my strength by walking, until the hospital called and told me that one of my pre-op exams had found that my kidneys were *off*. It had been very hot that June, and I had become dehydrated. They told me to stay indoors and to drink lots of water or the surgery would be canceled. I wanted desperately to have this procedure so I obeyed.

Finally, the day for my surgery arrived. I was called in to be internally cleaned by machines. I could see my insides on the computer monitor as they were being washed prior to surgery. Two longtime friends came to wait with Lynn.

I began to feel the terror of the last surgery. Should I, could I go through with it? Thoughts of canceling the surgery ran through my mind. I thought Lynn was going to strangle me. There was no way that she would allow me not to undergo this surgery.

However, as I was being prepped for surgery, I suddenly got cold feet again. What if the same thing that had happened in Montreal happened here while I was thousands of miles from home?

A Mexican American intern who was with me said, "We know your story. It was unimaginable what you endured, but Dr. Heppell is the best, and we all will be praying to God during this complicated surgery. Put yourself in the hands of the Lord." There are always angels around us when we least expect them!

Eight hours later, they wheeled me into the surgical ICU. When I awoke from the surgery, I put my hand up to my nose to feel for a tube, that would have indicated I was receiving treatment intravenously. As soon as I could feel that there was no tube, I was relieved beyond measure. Dr. Heppell, came in and told me it was over. He said that he had closed me and even worked with the kidneys to free them. He said, "Your creatine dropped immediately." This was the best possible news.

I kissed Dr. Heppell's hands and wished him, "Bonne Fête!" He laughed and said, "You are the only one who will remember that this is Quebec's national holiday!"

I must say something about the Mayo Clinic. When you enter the hospital, you might think you are in a first-class hotel. Someone is always playing the piano or the harp in the solarium. The cafeteria serves the best food in Arizona! Everything is spotless.

Of course, in our case, we were no longer American residents and consequently, had no insurance coverage in the United States, so Lynn paid by American Express. She had to pay up front for the surgery. It didn't matter whether you survived or not, it still had to be paid. We learned later that we were charged for *everything* I used—every pill, every Kleenex; even for someone to assist me in my walks. My bill was upward of one hundred thousand dollars before I left. The Metropolitan started to raise funds from the members of the archdiocese board of trustees, but when Lynn heard about it, she asked that it be halted. She felt humiliated.

Once I was back in my room, the order of business was to break wind. Once I passed gas, it meant everything was working properly. For the first few days, I had to adjust to the fact that I no longer had any appliances. I felt whole once again. I was amazed at just how wonderful it felt! We all take the most elementary bodily functions for granted until they are compromised.

I started walking, as quickly as I was able, and when the first bowel movement arrived, friends and relations all over North America were called with the news. It was funny to hear people celebrate this first sign of normalcy. Lynn, who was cooking a

Lebanese dish for the Ghiz family when I made the first call, gave a loud, "Whoopee!"

After several weeks, Dr. Heppell released me from the hospital. In his opinion, I was progressing quite nicely. Sally Ghiz generously offered us her home and car so I could recoup quietly. She and her son David were real angels in this difficult period in our lives.

We settled into their lovely Scottsdale home but not for long. The MRSA came roaring back. They rushed me back to the hospital. At first, the admissions personnel gave us a hard time because we still owed forty-five thousand dollars on our bill. Our American Express card was maxed out. This was late on a Friday afternoon, and with the time zone difference, Lynn could not contact anyone in Montreal.

The woman in Admissions said, "Well, when you buy a lettuce you have to pay!" Lynn retorted, "So my husband is a vegetable?" The Ghizes brought a check, and Lynn asked, "If he dies, now that he has been lying here in agony while you get paid, can I have my money back?" The local church pastor, Father Chris Salamy, who was there, fell over laughing. Dr. Heppell intervened and ordered my immediate admittance.

They finally rushed me into the ER, laid me out, and poked holes in my belly. Water gushed out. As soon as possible, they took me into surgery, laid me on the table as if I were on a cross, and told me not even to breathe. They were going into my jugular vein again with medication to kill the raging MRSA, which could have ruined the whole surgery and, quite possibly, killed me.

My tears flowed. "Am I ever going to get out of this unending descent into the black hole?" I was in a real panic, but thank God, this medical/surgical team treated me so delicately and did all they could to soothe my spirit.

Once they had medicated me, they returned me to my room. I stayed at the Mayo Clinic until the infection subsided and the wound was closing. They put a kind of medicated string in my belly button that had to be eased out a little at a time.

By the time I left the hospital a few days later, it was my birthday. David, my family, and some friends took me out for a little supper. *Am I getting back to normal life?* I wondered. These were the first tentative steps.

We stayed in Arizona until Dr. Heppell authorized me to return home. By now, it was the end of July. Our plane tickets had lapsed, and Lynn was trying to find a way to get us home through Stephanie Betros, my secretary at the time, who throughout the whole period of my illness had kept the church office running smoothly.

Finally, the church sent us tickets for the flight home. The ride was long, and the planes were crowded. We had to change flights, find wheelchairs to avoid my walking, and take care of our luggage. I had to have constant fluids to avoid dehydration. It was a nightmare flight, especially since I was still so weak from all the many procedures and medication.

In Montreal, Lynn wheeled me out of the airport, and we were greeted by the office staff and Zach Cattiny, our council chairman.

They drove us home that Saturday evening, and I couldn't wait to get into my own bed after two months in Arizona.

In Arizona, everything had been on one floor. When I got into my bed, I fell into a deep sleep. At one point during the night, I woke up and walked out of our bedroom. I was disoriented and fell over the banister from the second to the first floor. Luckily, my body was relaxed or I could have broken my neck. Lynn ran to help me get back into bed. There I was, laughing and crying on the floor, as I told myself that I had not survived ten operations just to die from a stupid fall.

I awoke early Sunday morning and got ready for church over Lynn's vehement protests. I wanted the parish to know that I made it and was back. Crazy? Ego? Who knows. It was a mixture of madness, love for the church, and a personal disregard of what I had just passed through, and it caused Lynn angst for no reason. She was so upset that I did not heed her advice and remain home to rest I thought she was going to leave me alone in Montreal and storm off to our home in Vermont. She remained but fumed for several days.

Let us learn from the past to profit by the present, and from the present, to live better in the future.

—Unknown

CHAPTER 5

GOING FORWARD

I was on the road to recovery, and life began to feel normal again. After a month, the wound healed, and I even began, tentatively, to swim. God, to whom I offered a silent prayer of thanksgiving, had once again snatched me from the jaws of death. I gradually returned to pastoral life and to doing what I love best—helping people get through terrible times. I went to see Dr. Stein, my surgeon, who was pleased with the result of the surgery. Lynn pleaded with me to take it slowly, but nothing happens slowly in Montreal or at St. George.

About one thing I was sure: I was no longer the same person. What I had seen and experienced in 2003 and 2004 had forever changed my life, my perspective, and my philosophy. My main challenge was to begin to say, "No," to people. Before I managed to stiffen my spine, I went through a few difficult incidents, which nearly stopped me in my tracks.

I had kept up a rather heavy schedule dealing with a large parish and working for the archdiocese. I had to travel to many meetings with the archbishop and his advisors.

The Metropolitan Archbishop was under attack on the internet for his policy dealing with his auxiliary bishops, who were demanding more independence from his authority. I entered into the fray with both feet to defend not only my friend of nearly fifty years but also the sanctity of the archbishop's cause for unity in the North American church. This proved to be one of the most stressful periods in all my years as a priest. Much was at stake.

The attack on the Metropolitan came from a vocal minority who were challenging him to disclose complete information about the finances of the archdiocese as well as any personal wealth he might have accumulated. This was, in large part, generated by some who felt disenfranchised. Among the dissidents were new converts, who in my estimation had not fully integrated into the ethos of the church and it's hierarchical structure.

Some of the bishops tried to show their independence from central authority by instituting old traditions like encouraging long beards, wearing cassocks outside the church, and lengthening the worship services. In general, everything they tried to implement was anathema to Philip Saliba, the archbishop for many years who believed in the integration into North American life as did his predecessors from the beginning of the 20th century.

Later, he realized he had made a mistake, and reversed his original decision by which they had been granted a certain autonomy; they were relegated to the status as auxiliaries to the archbishop. Some resented this. Even the laity vented their spleen publicly on the Internet, which was eventually was shut down due to the damage it caused across the board by the acrimonious content.

Those of us who were loyal to the Metropolitan fought against this challenge to his authority, both here and in Antioch (Damascus), where the patriarch resides. This proved to be one of the most distasteful episodes in the life of our church and to me personally, both emotionally and spiritually.

Meanwhile, I worked on a new and expanded edition of an earlier work entitled, *Ancient Church on New Shores: Antioch in North America*. This had been published in 2012 and was a detailed account of the complicated history of the church in North America. The new edition contained a large archival collection of documents, which had not heretofore seen the light of day. This monumental work required me to ensure the accuracy of hundreds of documents dealing with the political history of the Church at the time of the spread of Antiochian Orthodoxy from the Middle East to North American, and its early days in North America. This account spanned several centuries and verifying the facts and documents took me several years.

I now realize and accept that the pace of my ministry must be reasonable. There can be no more twenty-four-hour workdays for me! I know God spared me for something. I cannot throw away this gift. My life must be a silent offering of sacrifice to Him. I can no longer take life and its gifts for granted.

Unfortunately, I did not always heed this. It seems that as soon as the pain receded, I took up where I left off. It's human nature. However, I felt, at the time, that my life no longer belonged to me but that I was there for others.

Someone asked me how I would define my ministry, which would soon be approaching its fiftieth year. I quickly replied, "People."

He retorted, "People; not God?"

To which I replied, "People are the reflection of God. By serving the people, one serves God; serve God and one serves the people." This summed it up for me.

Things on the health front had been relatively quiet for a spell until my compromised immune system kicked up its ugly head once again. I had maintained a heavy schedule of work in the parish. There can be no doubt that the difficult political situation surrounding the archbishop and the challenge to his authority took its toll.

There is always a price to pay for engaging too heartily in highly charged emotional situations. The price I paid was getting shingles/ zona. It was so painful that I thought I was being knifed to death. I was at my home in Vermont for American Thanksgiving in 2009 and could not reach a doctor until Monday. I had to ride it out with pain medication that would not affect my kidneys. The first sign was that I found a bump on my head in the middle of the night. Then the illness attacked the lower part of my body. During all of this, I maintained a hectic pace, moving along with the tidal wave. I had clearly not learned my lesson.

My next health crisis arose a year later. While I was in church for services, I felt a pain in my chest so great that I asked my cousin, Dr. Tom Saba, to take me to the hospital. The ambulance rushed me to the emergency room at St. Mary's Hospital where I had been only a week earlier.

There, Dr. Campbell, Tom's professor, was on call in the ER. He diagnosed me with pneumonia. However, after taking the prescribed antibiotics at home, my condition worsened. I hallucinated, fainted, and fell down. That night I fell into the hall closet and passed out. My skin was oozing water because I had such a high fever. Lynn called the ambulance. I was taken back to St. Mary's Hospital.

A week earlier, one of my parishioners, Dr. Nelly Tawfik, with whom I had been having supper, had seen that I was ill. She had called Dr. Campbell, who had also been her professor, and had given him a preliminary report about my condition. I was admitted to the hospital because she had called him for a consult, as she had been very suspicious about the chest pain I described.

The ER doctors quickly realized that I was in serious trouble. They placed me in isolation and told me I was having renal failure. The bile duct in my liver was failing, and I had fluid on my lungs and heart (pericarditis). So here we were again. Dr. Derek Rahal, cardiologist, friend, and parishioner told me I was headed for a cardiac arrest.

They put me immediately in a glass isolation room in the ER, so I could be monitored constantly. It seems that I had a virus that was shutting down my vital organs. A procession of doctors filed in and out of the room. Everyone else was restricted from entry. I had to be hydrated and catheterized. Every effort was made to keep my body fighting the insidious virus. I remained in this state for five days until I was stabilized.

Being in isolation in the glass room was unsupportable. It was impossible to sleep. I didn't have one minute of sleep in five days.

Not only the incessant tests to check the status of the virus but also the lights and the cast of characters in the ER prevented any repose whatsoever.

I commended my life to the Blessed Mother. At one point, the nurses could not draw blood from me. After an hour of poking, with my body looking like a pincushion, I yelled for them to stop. I later saw a Jamaican nurse and asked her to come to me. I turned my eyes to heaven and said, "Listen. I am your son, Mary. Please let her get my blood at the first poke." Sure enough, it worked. In the end, our lives are often in someone else's care.

After five days in the ER, I was moved to a room on a floor in which there was nobody under the age of one hundred. It was on the geriatrics floor. Even my bathroom was prehistoric. A female doctor came in to take my history, whereupon I called the ER and insisted on speaking to Dr. Campbell. I asked him to come up and see me and told him that I was not about to share my story with a new doctor or take any treatment except his. I also insisted on going home.

When Dr. Rahal consulted him, Dr. Campbell said, "Wow! I didn't know your priest could be so obnoxious. Nobody has ever been able to contact me in the ER!"

Dr. Rahal asked, "Did he get you to come up to his room?"

"Sure did!" answered Dr. Campbell.

Dr. Rahal responded, "This was a measure of Father's respect for you, that he only wanted you. And this is how he runs his very large parish."

Later, Dr. Campbell came into my room with ten interns to

listen to my heart and told them, "Be careful with Father Gabriel. He's known to have a temper." I'm sure he was glad to get me out of his hair when he finally released me!

We had planned to go to Vermont that Thanksgiving. As I left the hospital to go home, Dr. Campbell and Dr. Rahal agreed to let me go to Vermont if I would follow their strict orders and only if there was a hospital close by (which was the case). So Lynn wrapped me up in a blanket and took me to Vermont for American Thanksgiving and also to have a week off with complete rest, well away from the parish. I started a new period of restoration.

I realized that after each painful episode, which I should have seen as a learning experience instructing me to slow down, I had still managed to return to the old ways of doing business to the detriment of my well-being. I am convinced that my compromised immune system and weak kidneys contributed to the rapid deterioration that had taken place. I also cannot tolerate antibiotics. It took me eight weeks to recover the strength I had lost during this latest episode. However, I was determined to fight back through a regime of exercise to rebuild my system that had been so wounded by the virus.

Dr. Campbell suggested that instead of swimming, which could have been the source of the virus, I undertake cardio and weight training to build my strength. He said, "You still have not fully recovered from several years ago."

So I tried to take life more slowly, to sometimes say, "No," and to set limits, but I was not always successful. However, I did manage to have several years of better health, for which I am deeply grateful.

Lord, hear my prayer,

listen to my cry for mercy;

in your faithfulness and righteousness

come to my relief.

Do not bring your servant into judgment,

for no one living is righteous before you.

The enemy pursues me,

he crushes me to the ground;

he makes me dwell in the darkness

like those long dead.

So my spirit grows faint within me;

my heart within me is dismayed.

I remember the days of long ago;

I meditate on all your works

and consider what your hands have done.

I spread out my hands to you;

I thirst for you like a parched land.

—Psalm 143:1–6 (NIV)

CHAPTER 6

LESSONS LEARNED

By now, the Montreal winters had begun to take a toll on us. Because two of our children lived in the United States and I had begun to think of retiring, living in a warmer climate became my dream. The thought of not needing coats, boots, gloves, and hats for weather that could drop to ten degrees below zero Fahrenheit (about -23 °Celsius!) for days if not weeks was very attractive. The prospect of getting into a warm car for which I was not required to vigorously scrape an icy windshield, was almost irresistible.

The winter of 2014 was awful! I vowed I would not stay another winter in Montreal. The snow was so high I could not get into our driveway or put the car in the garage when I returned from an errand. It remained on the ground for months. I trudged through snow up to my waist, having had to park the car blocks away. Visiting a parishioner was a nightmare.

Then in June 2015, disaster struck again. We had hardly begun to hope that the worst was behind us, when Lynn who had been my rock when I had had surgery and throughout my recovery, received the devastating news that she had stage III breast cancer and required a bilateral mastectomy. At the same time, I was hospitalized for the third episode of kidney failure within six months. After consulting with our physicians, we decided Lynn should travel to Arizona where our daughter Tammy lives, to begin hormone therapy in preparation for surgery.

At this time, Lynn's brother David[11] was diagnosed with terminal colon cancer, which had spread to his liver. David's life had revolved around his work and caring for his mother, Janna. We visited him in Virginia, when possible, and tried to offer what practical help we could.

Janna was independent and very haute couture, despite her age. She still drove her car, shopped, practiced yoga every day, never went to the doctor, and believed in positive mental exercises to stay healthy. While David battled cancer, she looked after him. Then one day she had a stroke.

Lynn immediately left for Virginia to help restore her to health. Shortly thereafter, Janna decided to travel to Canton, Ohio, her hometown, to visit her sister Audrey. There, most unluckily, she tripped and broke her hip. Again, Lynn rushed to her side to assist her. For some months, Lynn, her cousin Jeanne, Janna's sister Laurice, her nieces and nephews, and I took turns doing everything possible to make their lives more comfortable. After David's death, we knew that we would have to make provision for Lynn's mother to live with us. We were blessed to have her with us until her death on May 2017 at the age of 97!

Lynn had cared for me during all my health crises. Now she

needed me. I made the decision, therefore, to retire from Montreal where I had served as a pastor and a community leader for close to forty years. First, I had to wrap up my work in Montreal and sell our home so we could make the move to Arizona. Our twins, Mark and Tammy, have lived in Tucson for some years. They insisted that they were ready to care for us in the winter years of our lives.

As soon as she arrived in Tucson, Lynn began her treatment to shrink the tumors. To my amazement, she was not to be hospitalized. I thought this was strange; unlikely, even impossible. On the day of the surgery, we brought her to the hospital at 10 a.m. for injections to her lymph nodes and then went to the surgical center. Lynn went into surgery while we waited until 7 p.m. when she was released to return home with a caregiver. This rapid release from the hospital arose from the fear of infections. So the hospitals in the United States were no different from those in Canada as far as C. difficile was concerned.

Janna's stroke and broken hip and her son's rapidly moving cancer combined to bring Lynn and I frequently back and forth from Montreal to Virginia so we could help during those very dark days, and made 2015 a year of upheavals and challenges. We also trekked back to Tucson to embark on our new life.

Lynn and I are now in a *honeymoon* phase. This is a new time in our life with yet another challenge to be conquered with God's grace and our sheer willpower, as she battles cancer.

Life only demands from you the strength you possess.
Only one feat is possible—
not to have run away.

—Dag Hammarskjöld, *Markings*

PART 2

THOUGHTS FROM A WOUNDED HEALER

CHAPTER 7

REDEMPTION

It occurs to me that writing my account of the past few years has been cathartic for me. As I awoke from the coma, I scribbled random thoughts and recollections of nightmares on scraps of paper. These thoughts and recollections were especially useful when I addressed audiences on near-death experiences. They now help me deal with current crises that affect our lives.

When I began writing this book, I realized that I had changed completely. It took some time to understand that I had made it through all I had endured. However, when I did, it was a complete awakening of my soul. I knew that life would never be the same after facing death.

I was sensitive to others before, but now my mission is to exert every fiber of my being to reach out to others in a way I have never done before. When that nurse told me that I still had a mission, she was right.

My secretary, Viviane Gideon, called me a "witch" because I knew instinctively when someone needed me and would call that person. The person would often either say he had been about to call me or would ask me how I knew she needed me. I just knew. Even during chemotherapy, I called others in the church who suffered from cancer. Later, we started a cancer support group at the parish. It was as though my *sensitivity antenna* was heightened. Parishioners were amazed at the intuition that brought me to their homes or hospital beds. I just knew when someone needed me. On a personal level, my suffering allowed me to feel Lynn's pain and to rise to the occasion as caregiver.

Suffering gives us another point of entry, a third eye, an openness to others and their struggles and the chance of redemption. I have been granted another chance to tell others what I have learned about living life to the fullest, the power of faith and prayer, the joy found in music and the arts, in overcoming obstacles that come when we are most vulnerable, and most importantly, the power of love and forgiveness in healing.

Despite or because of all the troubles I have undergone, I want to convey a message of hope and courage to patients and their families. The support received from loved ones makes a great deal of difference to the person who faces a life-changing health cataclysm. I pray that my wound, which was open for all to see, inspires the reader to see the vital ingredients needed to live a rich life full of faith, hope and love, with all its valleys and peaks.

I have learned that healing starts from within and requires kindness to others and particularly, to oneself. Mostly, I have come to understand that when we are suffering, God's grace can comfort us in unexpected ways and through unexpected acts of kindness. We must recognize the kindness of others as evidence of God's love.

We must know that when we are severely tested, we need to learn the lessons that God gives us. The silence of the long nights I spent in a coma, the endless days I was in dialysis, the waiting, and the fear have all opened the doors to my soul, if I can only listen and learn.

> We are healed of suffering only by experiencing it to the full.

—Marcel Proust, *Remembrance of Things Past*, Part 2, *Cities of the Plain*

Without spirituality one cannot survive the *"curves"* that come our way. When I left the hospital, and returned home after four months of silence, I sat in my study, the walls of which were covered by ancient icons, and read the Psalms. The language of King David with his pleas to God became my language. I identified with the rhythmic beauty of the psalms, which enveloped me with musical, lyrical symmetry. A person could be swallowed up in their beautiful cadences like ocean waves rocking one to-and-fro, comforting and drawing away the pain.

When we read the psalms, it is amazing how each one is a jewel of supplication, prayer, and hope. Even though they were written long ago, they are as relevant today as they were then for a heart that anguishes and throbs in expectation of reconciliation, healing, and peace. The words, "Lord, I cry unto thee," pierce our hearts and quite simply identify with our suffering and longing. The psalms elevate the soul to new heights.

This was why I spent so much time listening to sacred music

and reading the Psalms for my very survival. It was here that God spoke to my heart and uplifted my spirit so I could fight on. As I passed through the desert of suffering, the scales fell from my eyes as a vision of healing waters appeared just ahead.

These reflections came to me during the time I went through acute kidney failure. I had to go into that place, *deep within the deep* of me, to deal with this traumatic experience during my days in isolation. The beautiful and sonorous language comforted my parched soul and gave me hope.

When our spiritual thirst is quenched, we receive a peace that surpasses all human understanding. What follows this peace is the outer layers of our egos being peeled away. Everything becomes transparent. We develop the ability to perceive reality as it truly is. There is no longer any place other than *the God within*. Ordinary human frailties, such as anger, pride and other negative responses disappear.

As a clergyman, I became a *wounded healer*, who had been scared and buffeted. I no longer looked at things on a surface level. The dimensions of depth replaced all superficiality. We plunge into the depths of oblivion to rediscover the *pearls of great price*, which are our hearts.

My whole ministry changed and redirected itself to reach out to cancer patients, grieving persons, and anyone who needed a touch of grace in his or her time of need. We had lost a granddaughter and a nephew under tragic circumstances. In these tragedies, there came acceptance. I know because I know. Cancer survivors speak their own language, for the proximity of death awakens them to the realities of life.

As I reflected on all I had undergone, I developed a new hierarchy of values. I found this involved a radical change in my lifestyle. The answer was no longer found in material objects or pursuits. Life took on a different color. Being part of a community became important. I had discovered this in the Montreal church community and now at Tucson's Holy Resurrection Church. There is no substitute today for the warm, loving companionship of fellow believers and family. Community is vital for our survival. Reaching out and helping others in need is redemptive as well as healing.

A *rule* of prayer, which is plain talk with God, means taking a moment to lift up the heart (the seat of the soul) to divine energy. One must find a silent, sacred space for this conversation. I think of it as the simultaneous ascent of the soul and the descent of the Spirit. This is, or can be, a moment of inner transformation. One result of my time in a coma was this form of meditation, which became my daily way of communicating with God. Anyone can do it. You can use the name of Jesus or say "God, have mercy on me" while synchronizing your breathing in rhythm with your little prayer. This simple act can completely change the texture of your day or evening and provide a sense of calm and centeredness.

When we go through suffering and overcoming, we can experience moments of rebirth in which we see the sunrise and sunset with new eyes. Forgiveness can and must flow through our veins, releasing all negative memories, such as past or present relationships and events, so they may be consigned to oblivion.

"Today is the first day of the rest of my life."[12] Those who are suffering can either be victims or victors. By faith in Jesus, we are all victors!

Now faith is the substance of things hoped for,
the evidence of things not seen.

—Hebrews 11:1, KJV

CHAPTER 8

SPIRITUAL WATERS IN THE DESERT OF FAITH

Here I would like to offer some contemplative notes, which have been born out of the crucible of suffering and faith, and some notions we should never forget. In my case, my experience caused the scales to fall from my eyes. The outer layer of my being peeled away so my soul could emerge from the depths and move toward redemption by grace and my life-long struggle with God.

A few times in my life, I have found myself riveted to one spot. Once on a beautiful autumn day, I visited an elderly gentleman, Mr. Merhige, who lived with his daughter in Sainte-Thérèse, Quebec. As I left his house, the sun was setting. It lit up the golden leaves of the tree in front of the house and shone through them, a ball of blazing, glorious fire.

I called the Merhiges outside to share this extraordinary sight with me. We remained transfixed by the scene for over an hour. We must be attentive to these signs and these moments. Even holy persons proclaim that nature is the fingerprint of God.

Another time, when I was in Lebanon, I went with Father Thomas Ruffin and Father George Shalhoub, who were longtime friends, to pay homage to the nuns who had prayed for my recovery from cancer. I visited the famous convent called the Saydet el Nourieh (Our Lady of the Light) Orthodox Convent near the village of Hamat, Lebanon. My friends and I spent the afternoon with the nuns, enjoying lunch and answering their questions about the church in North America.

As we were leaving the convent, which was situated at a high elevation overlooking the Mediterranean, I looked out and saw the blazing sun kissing the waters, again in the most powerful illumination. The sun's rays blazed across the sky, leaving us transfixed by the golden site. It was an unimaginable beauty created only by God. We watched until the sun sank into the Mediterranean, leaving its warmth in our hearts. Dostoyevsky famously said that we are saved by beauty, and at that moment, we were enraptured by God's beauty.

As I was writing this book, I realized that I had changed completely. It took me time to realize that I was still alive and that I had endured. Now I know that what I experienced was a complete awakening of the soul. I am free, leaving behind the carapace of self I had hidden behind to shelter myself from the world. Now, I could finally see my place in the universe and feel the gratitude of a survivor. In reaching out to others as I had never done before and in confronting death, I believe I have found myself.

There is that resilience that all one has is "the now", The past is gone, the future is unknown. Therefore, one must do the right thing with the ones one embraces in "the now".

The wound is the place where the Light enters you.

—Rumi

The *sursum corda* is a prayer found in the liturgy of all Christian churches, in one form or another. It exhorts us to let grace fill our hearts. Grace is the precious sense of gratitude and unconditional love each person experiences when he is in harmony with himself, with others, and with the creative power that created the cosmos.

It says, "Let us lift up our hearts!"

The congregation responds, "We lift them up unto the Lord."

For those of you who are in physical or spiritual pain, I urge you to take what I have learned to heart and to consider the thoughts and understandings that may resonate with you and your own situation. May these reflections bring you the peace that passes all understanding and the redemption we all seek.

I leave you with a few thoughts on the new, transcendent awakening that I have described.

God creates within our soul a mystic sense of wonder.

When you find beauty and wonder in those around you, you open the door of your heart to find the beauty in yourself.

Silence is the ultimate harmony in divinity, that is, God.

For a brief moment, I enjoyed the ecstasy of this beauty!

Watch clouds and winds

    and earth's living things

        unfold

            each day.

                A miracle!

Life by itself is a minute.

As the psalmist says, "This is the day the Lord has made. Let us rejoice and be glad."

Psalm 118:24 (ESV)

One cannot count the stars,

    nor touch them.

But in the magic of the night

    I feel their calm and glory.

To feel the calm, one must embark on the path of forgiveness—of past wrongs, hurts, and broken relationships. The road to holiness is the long journey within to discover the "pearl of great price." Forgiveness is the beginning of the journey.

To paraphrase Kabir, you will be there what you are here; you will receive there what you have given here.

The wonder of it all ...

    how snowflakes form

        and float to earth

and cling to every tiny twig,

    each needle of spruce and pine,

until all is soft, white, and oh, so fresh.

Cut the ties that bind you.

Change is constant,

    new heights, new valleys.

Beauty is constant.

For God is beauty.

There is nothing, no one more beautiful than God.

On this Earth there is a oneness—a rhythmic flow of life

    through everything that lives.

Each has a birth,

    a purpose to fulfill.

    Each an end

    and then a new beginning.

For the spirit of creation

    has picked me up

    and set me free.

We may see the glory of God in a speck of sand. His glory is
immanent in all creation;

Open the eyes of your heart to behold its wonders.

Whether this is imagination or not,

    one never really knows,

    and it matters little,

      for in that moment,

      ecstasy holds the soul.

Love all creation, it is said

even the smallest creatures

God embraces the whole of creation

and most of all you are in

the palm of His hands.

This is the fulfillment of the

      promise of life.

Nothing can be destroyed—

      everything is being created.

As the great symphony of life

        goes on with one

            unwavering purpose

        to create what is to be.

To see the face of God is to see every human being.

"To love another person is to see the face of God."

— Victor Hugo, Les Misérables

Even St. John asks us how we can love God and hate our brother whom we can see, but love God whom we cannot see. (1 John 4:20)

In the poem "Ars Poetica," poet Archibald MacLeish writes:

"A poem should not mean

But be."

And God just is. It is for us to discover His love.

Live to learn to love.

Learn to love to live.

Love to live to learn.

So that you may live the life that you yearn.

—Rico Dasheem, *Without Borders*, 2014

The journey of conquering your afflictions or suffering is a spiritual one. It is a journey to love yourself even as God loves you!

There is no consolation for suffering except to consider it against the background of the "other world." And this, indeed, is fundamentally the only correct point of view. If this world alone exists, the everything in it is absolutely nonsense: separation, sickness, innocent suffering, death. But all these require a meaning in that ocean of life which invisibly washes the small island of our earthly being. Which of us has not experienced the breadth of other worlds in dreams, in prayer? When a man finds in himself the power to acquiesce in the ordeal sent him by God, he achieves great progress in his spiritual life.

—Alexander Yelchaninov, *The Way of a Pilgrim and Other Classics of Russian Spiritualism*

NOTES

1   Diverticula are small, bulging pouches, which can form in the lining
of the digestive system. They are found most often in the lower part of
the large intestine (colon). They develop when naturally weak places
in the colon allow marble-sized pouches to protrude through the
colon wall. If these become inflamed or infected, leading to severe
stomach pain, changes in bowel habits and nausea can result. Several
drugs are associated with an increased risk of diverticulitis, including
steroids, opiates, and nonsteroidal anti-inflammatory drugs. For
more information, see the Mayo Clinic website:

http://www.mayoclinic.org/diseases-conditions/drticulitis/basics/
definition/con-20033495

2   Sarcoidosis is characterized by collections of chronic inflammatory
cells (lymphocytes) typically found in the chest, eye, or skin. Half
of the individuals have no symptoms, and the disease is usually
discovered accidentally. Its cause is unknown, but it may be an
autoimmune disorder. The disease usually subsides spontaneously,
but it can also last for years with relapsing episodes. See:

http://www.nmihi.com/s/sarcoidosis.htm

3   This historic event finally took place seven years later at Montreal's
City Hall on November 2, 2010. It was a historic first for Montreal.
My partners were Rabbi Leigh Lerner of Temple Emmanuel in

Westmount and his leading layman, the late Victor Goldbloom, an eminent ecumenist. I hope this will become a model for other cities.

4   From Job 38:1, "Then the LORD answered Job out of the whirlwind" (KJV).

5   A colostomy is an opening in the belly (abdominal wall) that is made during surgery. The end of the colon (large intestine) is brought through this opening to form a stoma. Where the stoma will be on the abdomen depends on which part of the colon is used to make it. See the American Cancer Society: http://www.cancer.org/treatment/treatmentsandsideeffects/physicalsideeffects/ostomies/colostomyguide/colostomy-what-is-colostomy

6   The ileostomy is an opening in the belly (abdominal wall) that is made during surgery. The end of the ileum (the lowest part of the small intestine) is brought through this opening to form a stoma, usually on the lower right side of the abdomen. See American Cancer Society: http://www.cancer.org/treatment/treatmentsandsideeffects/physicalsideeffects/ostomies/ileostomyguide/ileostomy-what-is-ileostomy

Chapter 2

7   Creatine is an acid that supplies energy to the cells in the body. It is synthesized in the liver and kidney and is transported through the blood and taken up by tissues with high energy demands, such as the brain and skeletal muscle.

Creatinine is a waste product generated by muscle metabolism. It is considered a fairly reliable indicator of kidney function. An elevated creatinine level signifies impaired kidney function or kidney disease.

https://www.kidney.org/kidneydisease/understandinglabvalues

8   *C. difficile or Clostridium difficile* is a bacterium that causes mild to severe diarrhea and intestinal conditions like pseudomembranous colitis (inflammation of the colon). *C. difficile* is the most frequent cause of infectious diarrhea in hospitals and long-term care facilities in Canada, as well as in other industrialized countries.

See the website of the Public Health Agency of Canada:

http://www.phac-aspc.gc.ca/id-mi/cdiff-eng.php

9   On Holy Friday, John Rossy was discovered to have died during the night. He was a popular radio host and one of the men who helped me form the St. George Men's Club, a humanitarian arm of the parish. He was also one of my young and staunch supporters. He belonged to the largest family of the community and was much loved for his *joie de vivre* and sense of humor. The funeral was held on Easter Monday. It was a great celebration with thousands in attendance, but it was a terrible blow during my recovery.

10   The Feast of St. John the Baptist, the patron saint of French-speaking Quebecers, is celebrated in Quebec on June 24. It is a politically-colored celebration of Quebec nationalism.

Chapter 6

11   When he died, David was honored by his peers for his dedication to the State of Virginia and for his years of honorable service at Arlington Parks. David was adored by his nephews and niece and their children as well as his aunts and cousins.

12   John Denver. *Rhymes and Reason* (album). 1969.

ABOUT THE AUTHOR

No individual clergyman from the Antiochian Archidiocese has had greater impact on the church's image in Canada and the United States than Economos Antony Gabriel. He gained this opportunity by being the youngest student to enter St. Vladimer's Seminary at 19, graduating in 1962, and that year becoming one of the youngest to be ordained by the Archdiocese. To the benefit of communicants and of society at large, he marked his 54th year of church service in 2016. Focus of his service throughout North America in a half century was 40 years in Canada with the Diocese of Ottawa, Eastern Canada and Upstate New York. His birthplace is Syracuse, N.Y., where he attended Syracuse University.

Another of his significant tenures was in Chicago where he established the suburban St. George Church of Oak Park, and was active in many ecumenical and civic organizations including the Conference of Race and Religions. He also was priest at St. George in Phoenix and St. Elias in Toledo. and was responsible for the receiving of many fleeing Black September in Jordan. While in Chicago he gained scholarly recognition with certificates in Philosophy from the Dominican House of Studies, Urban Studies from the Urban Training Center and honors from St Vladimir's on submission of a Thesis on Ephraim the Syrian, as well as from the Lutheran School of Theology in Syriac and Greek studies under Professor Arthur Voobus, world famous Syrianologist. Syriac emphasis was of the Exegesis of Moshe bar Kepha's Lukan narrative at Oxford University.

In Canada he was a founding member of the Order of St. Ignatius of Antioch, and streamlined the Department of Convention Planning and Credentials. He established and for years lectured on the first course on Orthodox Mysticism, "Eastern Orthodox Mysticism and Contemporary Literature", at McGill University. It was such service that earned him elevation to Archpriest and Economos by Metropolitan Philip and Great Economos by Metropolitan Joseph.

He has organized Clergy Associations, including Action for Peace, with participants from Jewish, Christian and Muslim faiths. During the Uncivil War in Lebanon, he guided Christian-Muslim religious leaders responsible for the fast track into Canada for refugees fleeing the war, and was active in receiving 10,000 immigrants regardless of religion. In every city he gained attention for such issues by serving as moderator of many media events, hosting his own radio programs and appearing on many national television broadcasts of Holy Services in English, French and Arabic.

In Montreal he expanded a 500-family parish into over 1,000

families with multiple services to give solace to those in special need. St. Mary's Church in Montreal developed out of St. George, the oldest Antiochian parish serving persons from Lebanon, Egypt, Antioch and Palestine, as well as native born Antiochians and converts. So services are tri-lingual with English emphasis. A global Legacy Fund was established to continue his humanitarian organizations caring for the elderly, poor and afflicted, stirring community action whereby food, money, jobs and homes were supplied by parish members. His Syrian Refugee Program is a model in North America. A first in the Archdiocese was his Family Services project with a full time psychologist to serve pressing needs of parishioners. He has traveled many times on missions to the Middle East for Synodal meetings with the late Metropolitan PHILIP, the accounts of which have been published in THE WORD over the years.

Writing and publishing have been a major element in his life. His book, Gabriel's Dragons, was published describing his journey to recovery against all odds from metastatic colon cancer. He later wrote Silence, a Diary of Suffering and Redemption, chronicling his six weeks in a coma, kidney failure and a host of health obstacles. The Handbook for the Order of St. Ignatius was published under his auspices as the first National Chaplain. After 10 years of research, he authored a definitive history of the Antiochian Archdiocese, Ancient Church on New Shores: Antioch in North America.

For many years he lectured at the Antiochian House of Studies, tracing historical development of the Church, as well as pastoral issues and ancient Syriac spirituality. As chairman of the Antiochian Heritage Foundation, he raised public awareness of the heritage of the Eastern church, as well as raising funds for projects designated by the Metropolitan. As recipient of numerous awards for humanitarian work, he is listed in The Who's Who In World Religions. He received the Gold Antonian Medal from Metropolitan Philip and The Knights of the Cedars Of Lebanon. In recognition of his humanitarian work, the government of Canada awarded him the Silver and Gold Jubilee Medal from Queen Elizabeth, he received the Cross of the Cedar from Metropolitan Elia Karam, and was recognized by the Province of Quebec and the city of Montreal through the National Assembly.

He retired as the longest serving pastor in Montreal. He married Lynn Georges, the first female seminarian of the Antiochian Church, with whom he has three children and five grandchildren.

Made in the USA
Middletown, DE
09 November 2017